YAMAHA BAND ENSEMBLES

A collection of mixed ensembles that correlate page-by-page with the Yamaha Band Student

John O'Reilly
John Kinyon

The YAMAHA BAND ENSEMBLES are designed to parallel Book One of the YAMAHA BAND STUDENT. Each ensemble page is correlated to the method, thus enabling the teacher to easily find and reinforce those materials previously taught.

This ensemble folio will serve not only to motivate beginning band students in the classroom, but also to encourage home and neighborhood combos as well.

YAMAHA BAND ENSEMBLES can be performed by a wide variety of instrumental combinations.

Line A is always the melody part, to be used for solos.

Line B is always the preferred harmony part, to be used for duets.

Line C is always the bass part, to be used for trios and/or full band ensembles.

In the percussion book. . .

Line A is played by keyboard percussion.
Line B is accessory instruments.
Line C is snare drum and bass drum.

A simple but effective piano accompaniment is provided in the score.

Contents

Instrumentation

Flute/Oboe
B♭ Clarinet/Bass Clarinet
E♭ Alto Sax/Baritone Sax
B♭ Tenor Sax
B♭ Trumpet/Baritone T.C.
Horn in F
Trombone/Baritone B.C./Bassoon
Tuba
Percussion
Conductor's Score/Piano Accompaniment

YAMAHA®
is a registered trademark of
Yamaha Corporation of America

Music Engraving by Sheldon Music Service, Inc.

Page 2 in students' books.
Correlates with page 6 of the
YAMAHA BAND STUDENT, Book 1

Playing Around

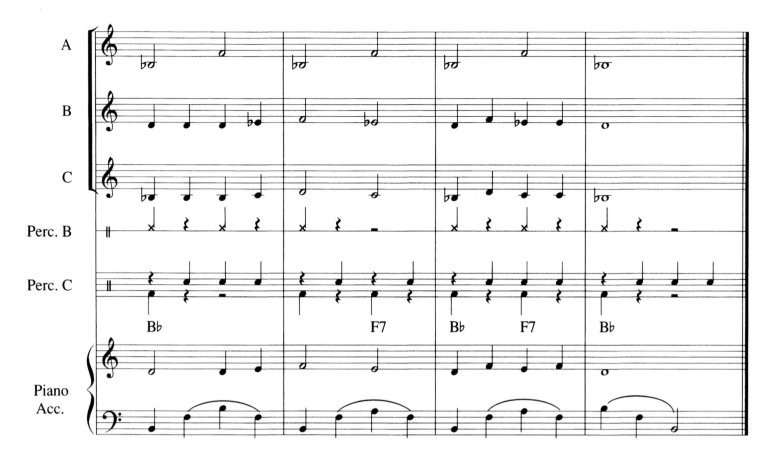

Page 3 in students' books.
Correlates with page 6 of the
YAMAHA BAND STUDENT, Book 1

Tisket a Tasket

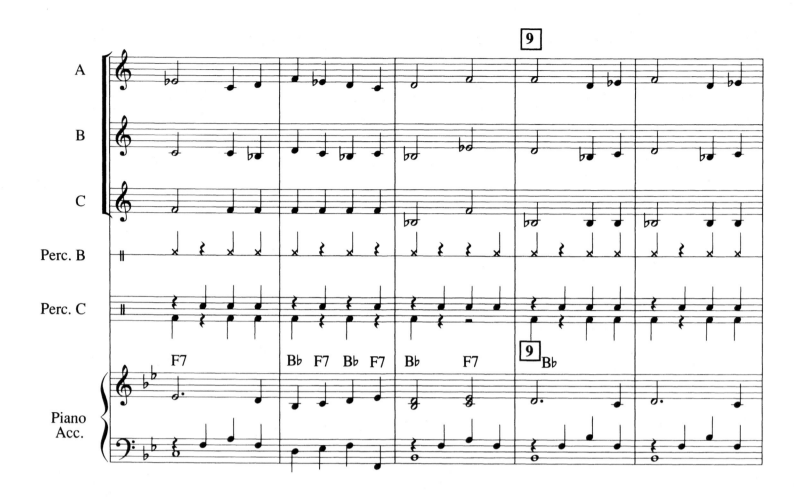

Page 4 in students' books.
Correlates with page 7 of the
YAMAHA BAND STUDENT, Book 1

Star Chase

Up on the Housetop

Page 5 in students' books.
Correlates with page 10 of the
YAMAHA BAND STUDENT, Book 1

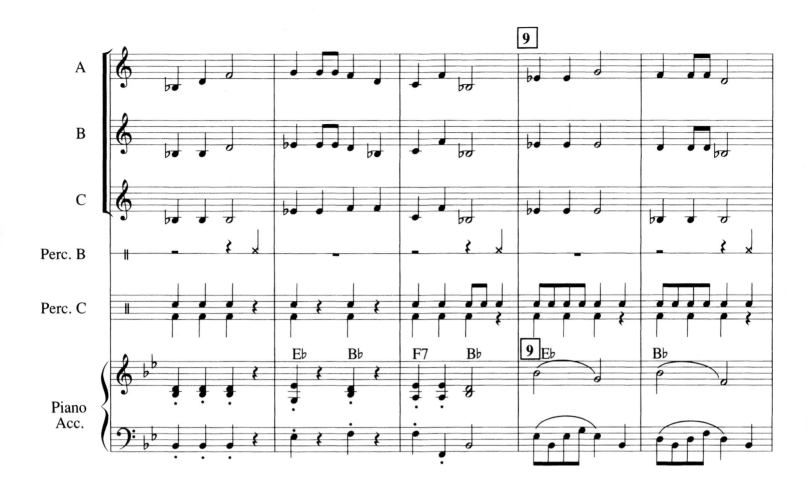

Page 6 in students' books.
Correlates with page 11 of the
YAMAHA BAND STUDENT, Book 1

Irish Folk Dance

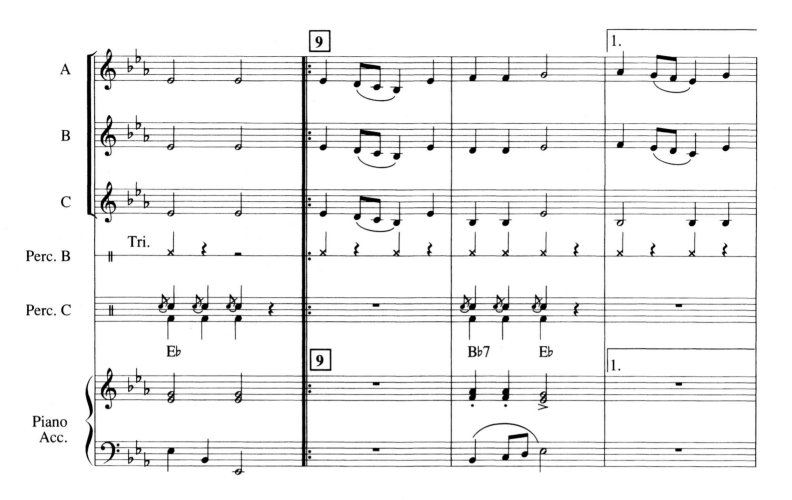

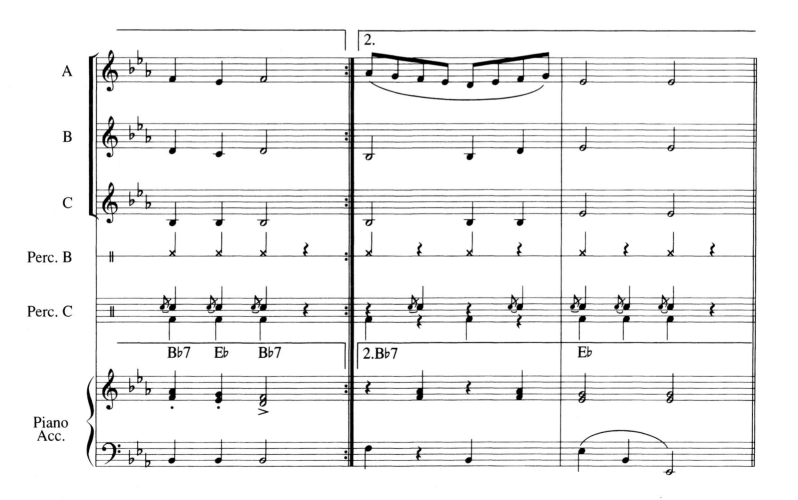

Page 8 in students' books.
Correlates with page 12 of the
YAMAHA BAND STUDENT, Book 1

O Come All Ye Faithful

The Carnival of Venice

Page 9 in students' books.
Correlates with page 13 of the
YAMAHA BAND STUDENT, Book 1

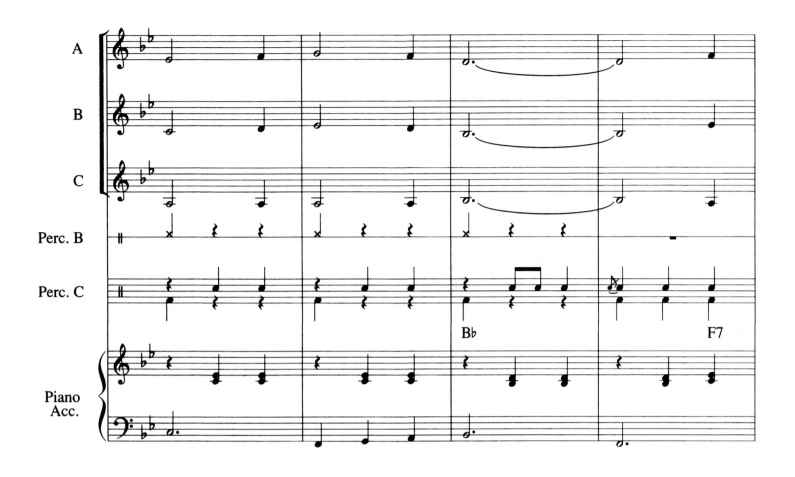

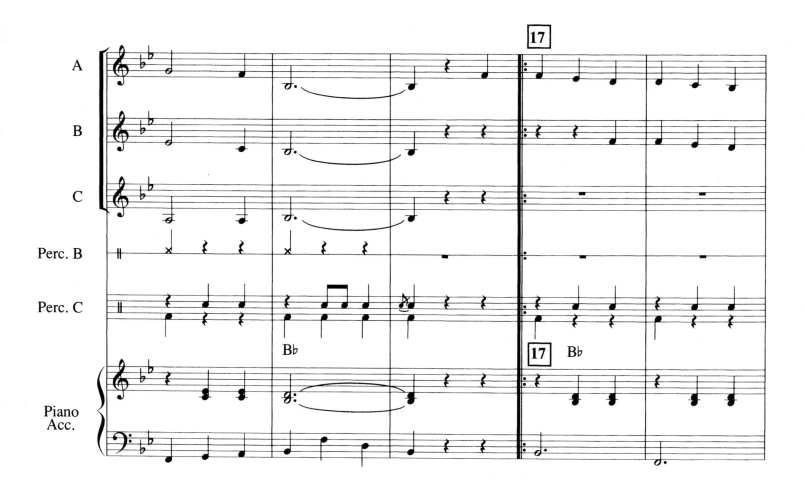

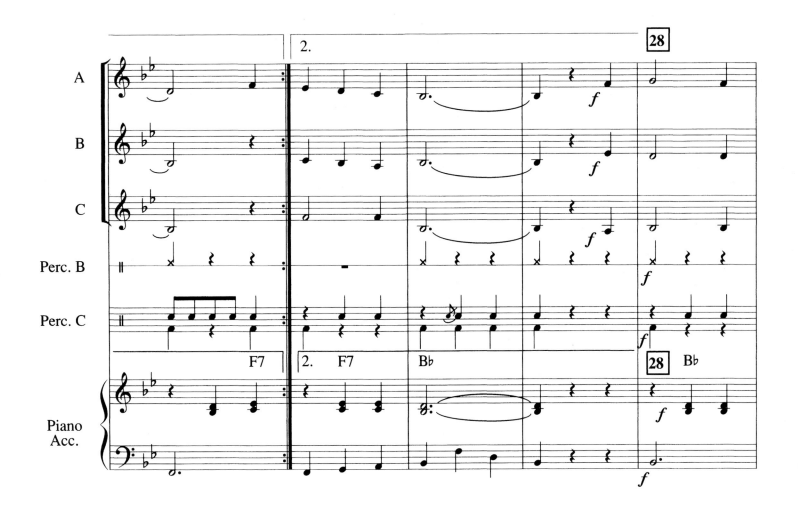

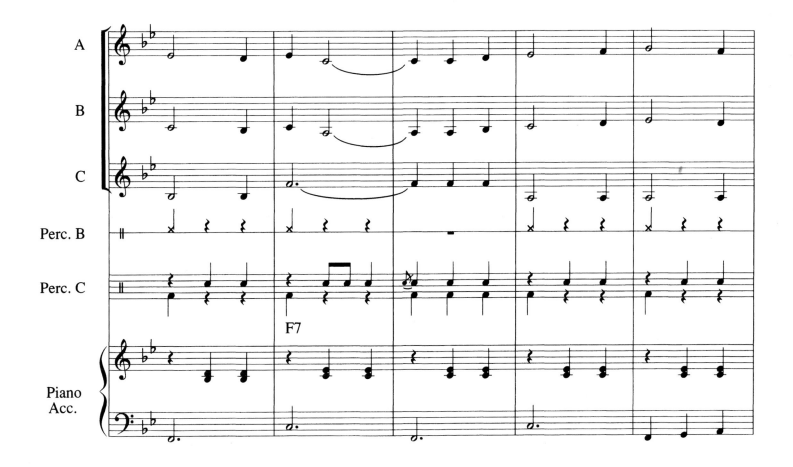

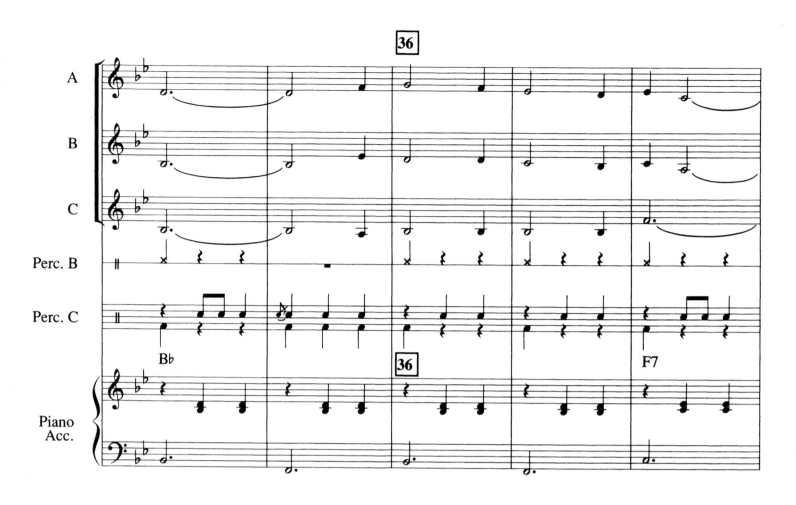

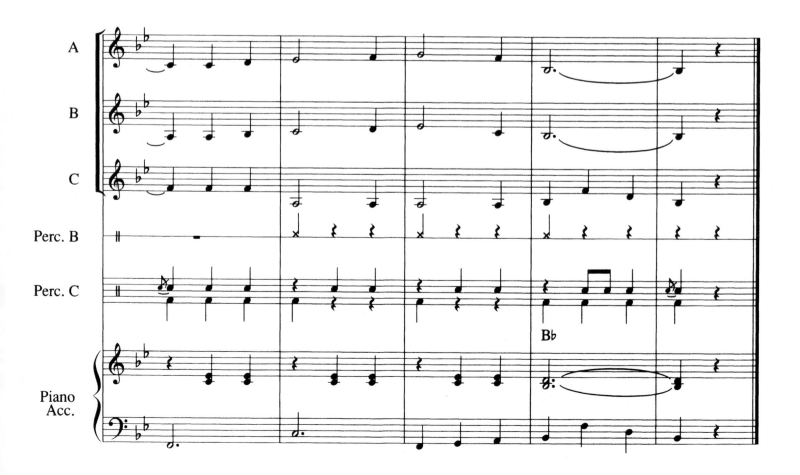

Page 12 in students' books.
Correlates with page 14 of the
YAMAHA BAND STUDENT, Book 1

Grandfather's Clock

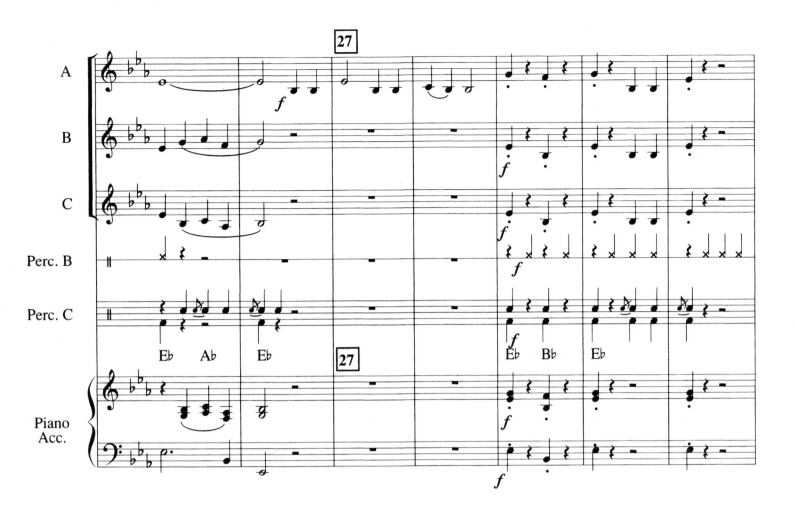

Page 14 in students' books.
Correlates with page 15 of the
YAMAHA BAND STUDENT, Book 1

Waltzing Winds

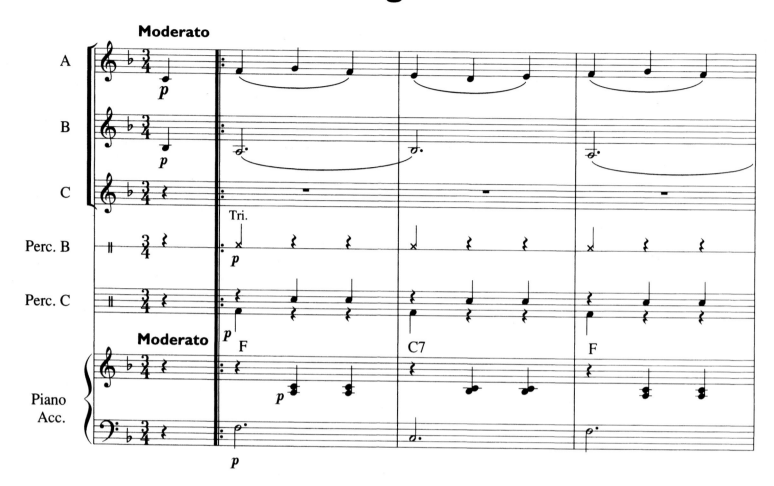

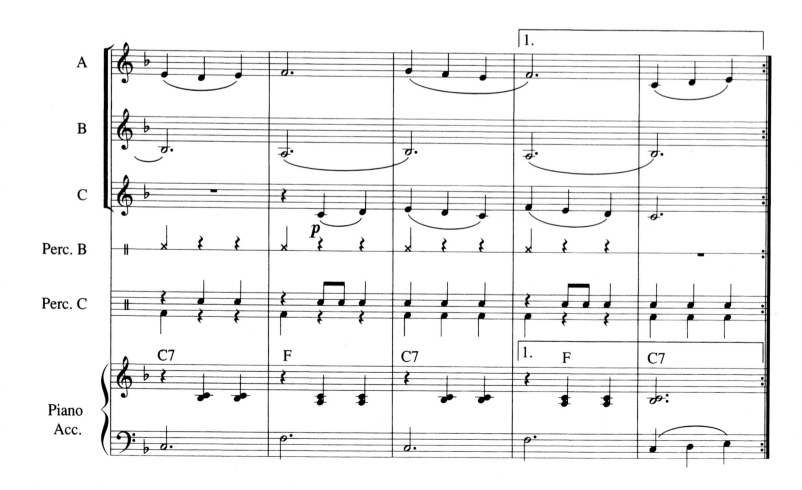

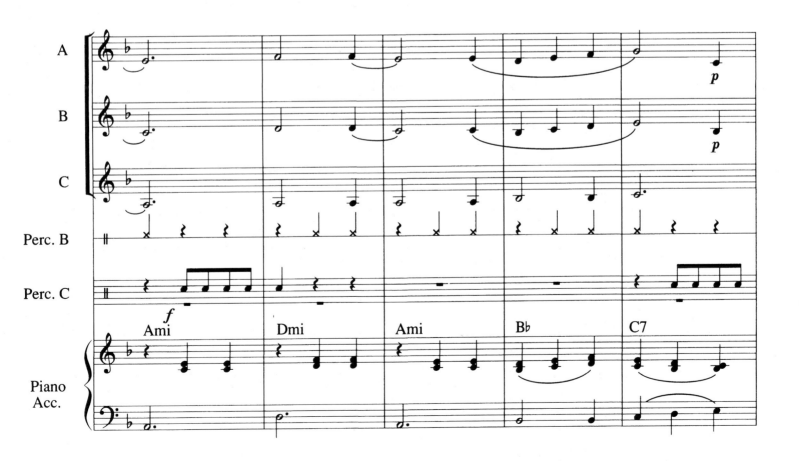

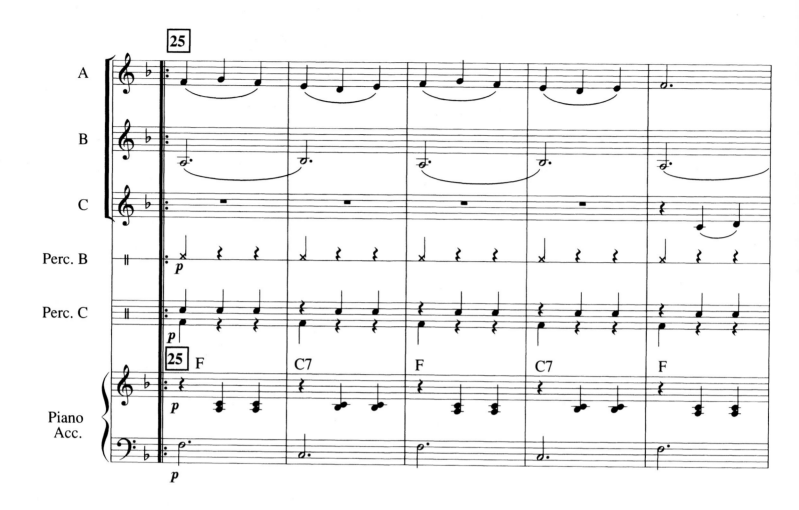

Page 16 in students' books.
Correlates with page 18 of the
YAMAHA BAND STUDENT, Book 1

Mini March

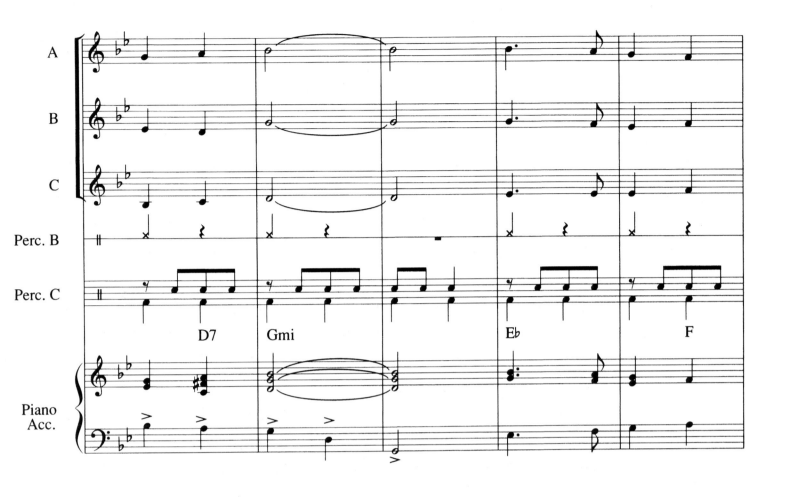

German Waltz

Page 18 in students' books.
Correlates with page 18 of the
YAMAHA BAND STUDENT, Book 1

Erie Canal

Page 19 in students' books.
Correlates with page 20 of the
YAMAHA BAND STUDENT, Book 1

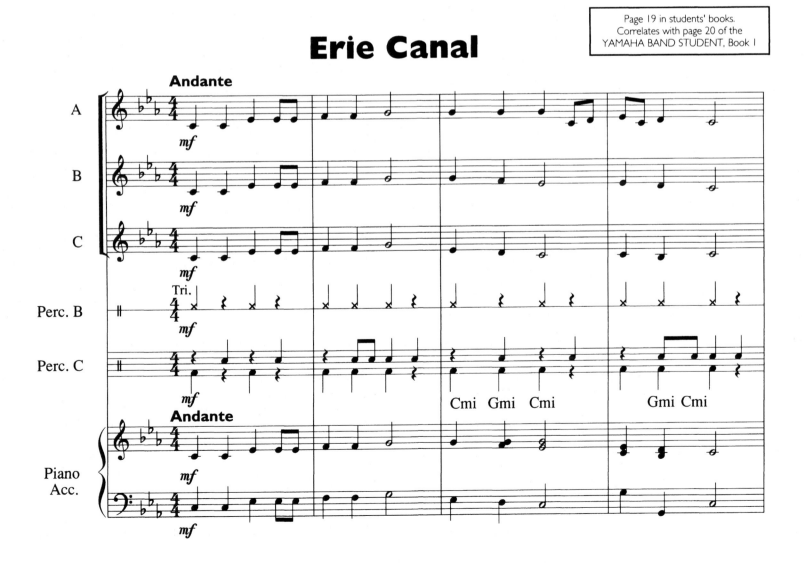

Page 20 in students' books.
Correlates with page 21 of the
YAMAHA BAND STUDENT, Book 1

Polly Wolly Doodle

Military March

Page 21 in students' books.
Correlates with page 23 of the
YAMAHA BAND STUDENT, Book 1

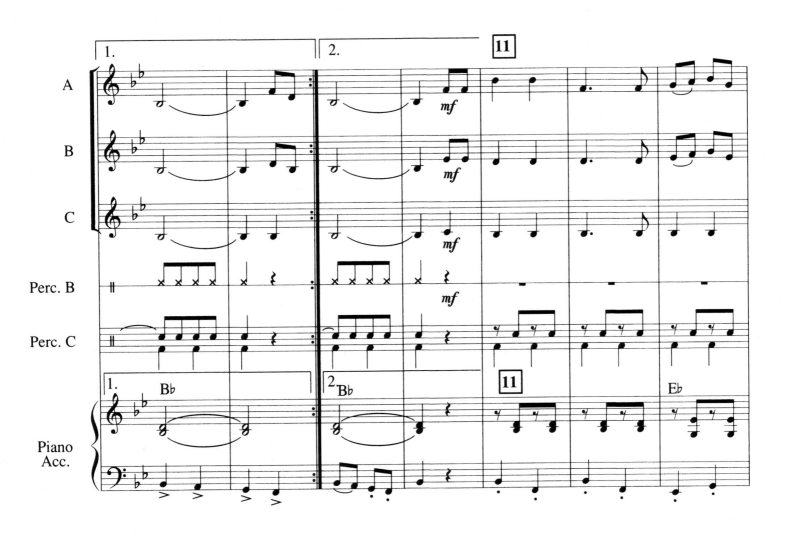

Page 22 in students' books.
Correlates with page 25 of the
YAMAHA BAND STUDENT, Book 1

Serenade

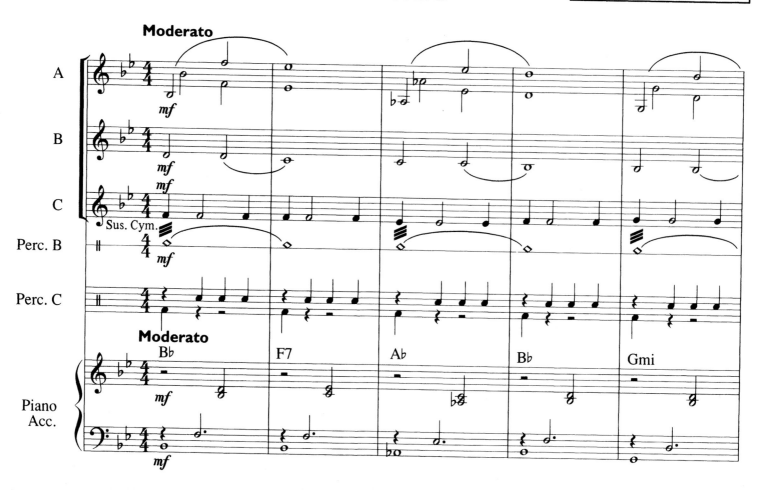

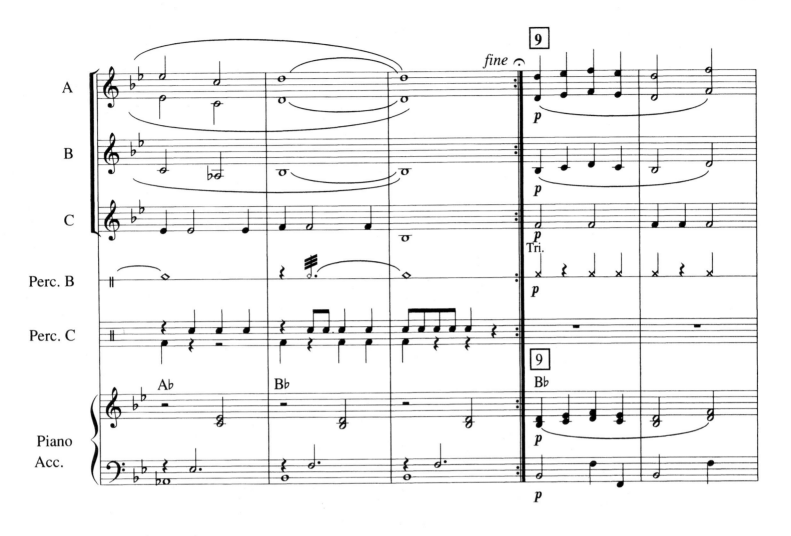

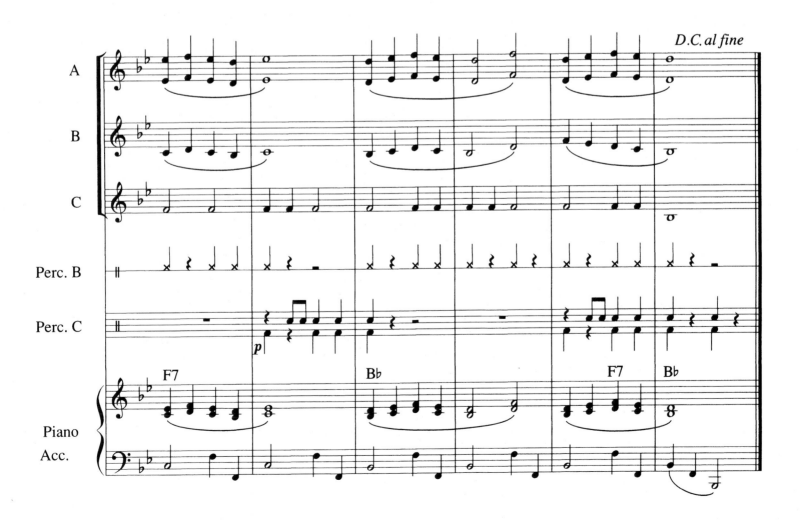

Page 23 in students' books.
Correlates with page 27 of the
YAMAHA BAND STUDENT, Book I

Song of Thanksgiving

Page 24 in students' books.
Correlates with page 28 of the
YAMAHA BAND STUDENT, Book 1

Rock a Bye Baby